#NousSommesParis

#Nous Sommes Paris

AN EYEWEAR SPECIAL EDITION
EDITED BY **OLIVER JONES**

First published in 2016
by Eyewear Publishing Ltd
Suite 333, 19-21 Crawford Street
Marylebone, London W1H 1PJ
United Kingdom

Typeset with graphic design by Edwin Smet

Printed in England by Lightning Source

ISBN 978-1-911335-46-7

Eyewear wishes to thank Jonathan Wonham for his generous patronage of our press.

WWW.EYEWEARPUBLISHING.COM

To all those in Paris,
and to all those who love Paris

TABLE OF CONTENTS

9 BEFORE AND AFTER BATACLAN

11 SURELY IT IS NO TIME FOR POETRY

15 DESPITE THE FISTS AND STONES, WE GROW

16 GARGOYLES AT ST GERMAIN L'AUXERROIS

17 SCREAM

18 EMPTY PARK GRAY

20 IN PARIS BEFORE THE WAR

21 SHOULDER TO SHOULDER

22 STRAIF

25 THE BICYCLE

26 BATACLAN

27 THE BOW

28 YES, THE LIGHTS

30 NOUS SOMMES PARIS

31 UNDER BLACK

32 FRIDAY THE THIRTEENTH

33 LE PAVILLON DES LETTRES

34 THE POINT OF PAIN

36 SLOW MOVING SORROW, FRIDAY 13TH, PARIS

39 BIOGRAPHIES

#NousSommesParis

BEFORE AND AFTER BATACLAN
ADELE FRASER

Everything gets filtered
through experience.
At first,
   they believed the shots
were fireworks. Just part of the act.
A display. A game. Something safe
and familiar they'd known in their old lives,
back in a time when they hadn't the history
to recognise the sound
of gunfire.

Now,
   new years will find them
launched into a new world,
where rockets will trigger
experience-instilled instincts,
and they will blanch and tremble
at the bangs.
Anxious acquaintances
will reach out
helpless hands,
attempting to hold them
securely in the day
and away from
memories.

In response, they will aim to readjust
their faces, so it appears
they're looking forward at the lights
and focused on the flashes
instead of the flash
-backs.

Only to those who stand the closest
will they whisper
their guiltless confessions.
'I thought it was...
I thought it was...'

Terror.

SURELY IT IS NO TIME FOR POETRY
GEORGE HOBSON

Surely it is no time for poetry.
How dream when murder stalks
here there everywhere
                    murder
and the wind in the pines coming off the sea
carries only moans of the dying,
wails of the mourning?
How be enraptured by oleander flaring on roadsides
when each bloom is a rocket exploding
and the leaves are long knives cutting throats?
How grieve over personal loss
old age
the evaporation of the past
when everywhere and daily and always
are bombs/craters/body-parts
eruption and corruption
whole populations scattered by greed
raped/ravaged/ruined
fleeing the destruction of everything theirs
the debris of what was ordinary life
now just smashed brick and charred wood?

All that is local, rooted, wild, old,
is going down before hubris
and being buried with millions of bodies
no one has use for.
Humans are mutating into flies
buzzing everywhere and nowhere
landing/leaving
here/there/nowhere
soiling window-panes that look out on sky

leaving black specks on tablecloths
depositing maggots in carrion
and the rubbish heaps of cities
where rats and vermin live
and human beings no one has use for.

We have asphalted space
and sterilized time.
Today is great with nothing,
feeding on illusion.
The air is poisoned
and we have no time to breathe anyway.
Only blasted trees and preposterous towers
scratch the horizon of the future.

Surely it is no time for poetry.

I no longer hear the sound of the cricket,
the frog no longer croaks by the pond at night,
the crow has stopped cawing.
The white wolf will not lead its pack again
across the frozen snowfields of the north.
Ice-floes shrink,
permafrost softens,
the home of the polar bear is melting.
Sea-birds trapped in oil-spills suffocate,
the ocean floor is poisoned.
In lakes foul weeds riot,
fish go belly-up.
Wild forests fall to the saw,
yellow metal monsters gut mountainsides,
orange flames turn prairies black.
Deserts eat up green land,
plagues bloom like algae in rivers,
insects hopping/crawling/flying
                              are on the march.

In a zoo in a city somewhere
a Bengalese tiger without offspring
paces up and down in its cage.

Nature is unnatured.

Black is perpetrated and called white
or just is perpetrated and called nothing

Greed rules
murdermurder
Women strive to keep order and scavenge and are raped
murder
Children are born old or ill
they are orphaned/abducted/seduced
they shoot real guns
sold by snakes and spiders
murdermurder
Untimely warmth deceives buds.
Politicians cry "Spring, spring", when there is no spring –
frost then massacres the blossoms.

The adder lies coiled at the door,
the black widow has crawled into the house,
the scorpion lurks between the sheets of the bed.

Surely it is no time for poetry.

To the contrary –
surely it is a time for poetry.
When night falls, and the far-off beat
of drums draws near, we shall sing God's Life
and ours, defeating darkness with our words.
Like rain-clouds arising in blue sky,
full of water for the desiccated earth,

our words arise in the heart of the Word
who makes all things out of silence.
It is time to speak, to cry out, to create.
We shall send our words in legions
against the raiders of villages
and the bombers of cities
who destroy the habitations of men
and slay women and children.
We shall praise the Creator,
who makes and re-makes being
and all beings existing.
We shall lift him up in the teeth
of the snarling wolf and the hissing viper,
and they shall wither at his sight.
Words spoken out of light
are greater than drums beating
at night in the jungle:
life-bearers,
they carry God's power,
they carry *hope* –
and by *hope* in our Creator who is faithful,
we shall stand.

Surely it is a time for poetry.

DESPITE THE FISTS AND STONES, WE GROW
GEORGE SYMONDS

A fist needs blood to keep on pumping, keep
its fingers pink. Some stones have blood within.
The fist caressed the stone. The stone lay cold.
Pretended death. The fist then smashed the stone
against its own forehead. The minerals
disaggregated, drew the fist's own blood.
Enraged, emboldened, sanctified, the fist
kidnapped the stone, to catapult to hell.
Abyss agazed, the stone became a fist.
It cut the air to strike the stones below.
For blood. And every blossom side a stone,
with kith uprooted, desolate and damned,
was torn by flying rock, or crushed by force
of blind, indiscriminate and thirsty fists,
unconscionable.

GARGOYLES AT ST GERMAIN L'AUXERROIS
ANNETTE SKADE

I lift the catch and they pour in,
springing from corbel and dripstone:
the squat dog with the head of a fish,
the baboon-faced dwarf,
legs wrenched to fit the capstone,
the long-haired madwoman
tortured mouth agape, spewing nothing.

Each morning when we leave I cannot shake them.
They wrap stone arms around my neck,
whisper and plead. In the evening they shuffle up,
beg me for alms. I drink them in with my wine.

They compel me to sleep in jumpers,
leave windows open wide.
You shiver too, to please me
but you are hard to gull.
Now you lean elbows on the window rail,
crane out from the room,
blow cigarette smoke into their very faces.

They strain towards you like the eager slaves they are,
the mouth-pullers, monsters, chimeras and grotesques.
These works of long dead labour, made lepers by time,
kiss the air by your cheek – once, twice, like Parisians do.

This poem first appeared in the *Shop Poetry Magazine*, Ireland, and in Annette Skade's
collection *Thimblerig*.

SCREAM
SIMON CARVER

So it is 2015 and here we are
In the future of the Twenty-First Century
All twiddling our thumbs and fiddling on and on in
The crazed dog heat of the Promised Land
While the Goths hammer at the gates and books burn
In a world forever mad with the rage of gods
Full throttle backwards into the rich odyssey of the New Millennium
Ever sidestepping hope to return to an age of plagues
With the dead and the dispossessed trailing
All the way to Mars
Lost in time and one great, impotent tweet
And there we have it
My dearest brothers and sisters
2001 and 2010 have been and gone
Leaving Moonbase Alpha far behind
Just four short years from *Blade Runner*
We look fully set
To boldly go nowhere
In a galaxy far, far away
Being so very much
One humanity
Out amongst the stars

EMPTY PARK GRAY
SANDRA M. GILBERT

winter-summer Paris
not a single kid in chic
Parisian overalls

& June blooms preen
for no one or for
drops of chill:

lobelias burrow
deep in blue
& clouds of pink

rise up from roses
globed & primped
to greet a dance of bees

that's just a dance
of absence under
hollow sky –

But look!
How there they are
those show-off roses

unfolding glowing
promise
for a missing audience...

Yet not far from here
the streets uncoil where
history will strafe

a few more bloody
fleurs du mort.

Square Leopold Achille, 2015

IN PARIS BEFORE THE WAR
WYNN WHELDON

The highest form of joy there is on this earth
is to make other people happy. – A. Hitler

In the Place Saint-Andre-des-Arts, they sit
sipping Pernod waiting for the day to end.
"I don't much care for Michelangelo,"
he remarks, apropos of nothing, merely
perhaps breaking a comfortable silence.
All afternoon had been spent in bed
and now they are relaxed, ready for the night.
But she is having none of his clatter:
"that I don't believe. You're much too grand for that."
"I don't like big things," he insists, smoking.
"You like elephants". "Ah, yes, I do, quite true.
I do like elephants. Though not in opera".
She sighs. She sips. She smokes too. Paris hums
and honks and cries. Two young Germans arrive,
take the next table. Their coats are so smart.
They chatter and chatter, pontificate on art.
In a gap he leans towards them, and
beckons like a drunk: "Ich hasse Herr Hitler".
The young Germans stare at the impertinence,
at each other, at him again, at her,
and then, infuriatingly, laugh. So,
in English: "What's so bloody funny, eh?"
Suddenly he feels sick. They were coming.

SHOULDER TO SHOULDER
KATE NOAKES

I do not ask why.
I deny you understanding
credence, acceptance.

Because, because, because.

I already know
you make no sense.

    ★

Je ne demande pas pourquoi.
Je vous nie compréhension
crédibilité, acceptance.

Parce que, parce que, parce que.

I déjà sais
vous êtes sans sens, sans sensibilité.

STRAIF
SALLY WILLOW

My name is
           wound:
               open
                      violence
              open   e trating
                    silence

write   wound   across my chest;
        scratches, marks in blood
                  in flesh

pull me screaming from the silence: word
        into this world of darkness
                  [my death: certified]

in blueblack ink
          suspension

      of time

                            [iron: gall]
                     the bitter stain
                        of words
                          piercing
                            fibres
                    of [my] flesh &
                        this world
                  to remain there
               more than death:

eternity

calling [me] into being

        calling [me] from [myself]

                like needle

sharp

        drawing [blood from]

           drawing [ink upon]

                my skin

immediacy of [my] death
is
      infinite

          space

              between

[my] past and
      [your] future

                  insert
              into that space
             the sly edge
            of thorn tip
             scribing

        [my] sang : [your] encre

spills   out   upon
        this flesh [wound]
         unbound
          liquid
          life

                    in habiting
                     in finite
                     space[s]
                    in between

[our] fate

and i see   i am
                          writereader
                             of this book

the spaces in between
                    [your] page and [mine]
                        in finitely
                        [un]bound

                                        [my] ink spills
                                            upon

[your] surface

word is   wound
blood is   silence:
        dreaming
            [re]creation
                         in its endless bloody violence

THE BICYCLE
JIM MACKINTOSH

Padlocked. Black and unsure like the Paris sky
at a point in the enforced sobriety of chaos,
a bicycle supports the weight of a single rose,
petal after petal wilting, never to be held.

Its owner dead among the dimming café lights
between the vastness of huddled innocence
and the visible spectre of cowardice. Haunted.
Not broken. Not surrendered. Reassembled.

The helicopters shadowing, counting, reporting
how they re-appeared in their thousands, nervous,
defiant, to reclaim the streets, to reset the tables.
A single rose on a table for two lovers, unbroken.

BATACLAN
ANDREW SHIELDS

We saw l'*Origine du Monde*; we went to Notre Dame;
we wandered down the Champs-Elysées.
We went into a bookstore, saw a cat with no name
and had coffee at a famous café.

Mona Lisa's still got the highway blues;
Napoleon's still in his grave.
We've paid up our tourist dues;
I need some time for a shower and a shave.

    It's been a long day in the City of Light;
    who's playing at Bataclan tonight?

We saw that place called Deux Amis;
Let's get tapas and a glass of wine.
That's what we are: we're *deux amis*,
on vacation and feeling fine.

    It's been a long day in the City of Light;
    who's playing at Bataclan tonight?

We'll sing along if we know the song,
and if we don't we'll clap our hands.
We've been walking the city all day long;
I just want to hear a couple bands.

    It's been a long day in the City of Light;
    who's playing at Bataclan tonight?

14 November 2015

THE BOW
CHRISTINA LUX

the two child prophets
rebuild the world from laughter
slide right down Noah's old bow,
sail above troubled waters
then over Rome: hands floating
then clasped, all moons at their feet,
clothed in sun, shining, no words,
k'auna, amore sans fin

YES, THE LIGHTS
MARGO BERDESHEVSKY

I would fill my mind with thoughts that will not rend.
(O heart, I do not dare go empty-hearted)... – Rupert Brooke

Yes, the Christmas lights hang ahead of the hearts.
The boots for war are sweating.

I know.
C'est la guerre. They said so then – They say so, now.

I don't know
What bandages to fold, what wounds to wrap.

I know, *c'est la guerre.* They said so then – they say so
Now. Burned breaths. Dry autumn, beneath.

There is an ancient tradition of filling the cracked bowl with
Gold – to honor what has broken. What is known. We have

Broken again. Blood-moon. Hunter moon. Ecliptic
Hour – like a hummingbird hung over the shoes of war

Standing still. Shared prayer, hear me.
I fear me.

Lights hung ahead of shrouds, *c'est la guerre,* but not
Yet – not now. Don't hear me.

Is Paris back to normal? No, darlings, not at all.
Not anything near normal, not at all. That, we know.

And no bomb of ours or of theirs and no gun will heal it.
Blood moon, hunter moon, filling our cracks with gold.

Will you fill our cracked bowl?

Fill it with a liquid for our vein of burned love.

Paris | November 2015

NOUS SOMMES PARIS
GREG SANTOS

At home
We hid under a desk
Outraged
Firebombed
Brutally threatened
Sombre
Darkest day
Disappearing

★

Bolstered
Pledge
Let us unite
Tell the media
Defend art
We will win
Waving pens and papers
Armed and dangerous
Final *coup de grâce*

Author's note: This poem was written using text remixed from a CBC News article on the *Charlie Hebdo* shooting on January 7, 2015.

UNDER BLACK
SOPHIE FENELLA

A decision made with shaking hands to hide the city
in black cloth, like the Jewish tradition to cover mirrors
in times of mourning. To see reflection is to know
life is living, to watch autumn hair reflect the sun
and keep breathing. To look in the mirror and see
black, is to see no life, no breath, moving in light.
I suppose the city is now a mirror, no glass is unbreakable.
Rain wet streets are prophecies, wet pebbles always slip,
and every crack in Regency terraces is a warning sign
or some ungodly omen of what's to come, all
two hundred buses falling on Christmas shopping streets
are worth Gladiator declarations of battle,
even if the battle will always be fought on troubled water.
A decision to stop a party with a black Toyota and a loaded
cry, don't take my tomorrow, reminds the city of its
glass-like structure, pavements are clay soft,
swallow running feet, brick houses crumble
in papier-mâché dust.
A decision to turn the city over, take cover in
its own roots, to shroud the morning in dust sheets,
sends schools spinning into double security lock down
as the lights go off, at Notre Dame.

FRIDAY THE THIRTEENTH
CAROLINE BRACKEN

We drank white wine, toasted the birthday girl
in a Dublin pub – a three-generation clan fest,
some MIA for unavoidable reasons,
gone to the other side
but thought-of, included in anecdotes.
We ate Thai beef salad, fought over the last scraps
of sun-dried tomato pesto, slagged the vegans
about you-don't-know-what-you're-missing steaks.
Between dessert and coffee, quiet conversations:
I'm here if you need me: Are you sure you're ok?
Parting with hugs, promises, linked arms
we teetered home, sated, safe.
In Paris, our night was reprised in *La Belle Equipe*,
another family, steak knives poised,
blood at their feet,
brothers shielding sisters,
the birthday girl's last candles
flickering.

LE PAVILLON DES LETTRES
ZATA BANKS

In the alphabet hotel I am sleeping inside a letter
A shape.
A word.
I am sleeping inside all of the colours containing this sound.
In the alphabet hotel I am sleeping inside a shape.
A word.
A colour.
I am sleeping inside all of the sounds containing this letter.
In the alphabet hotel I am sleeping inside a word.
A colour.
A sound.
I am sleeping inside all of the letters containing this shape.
In the alphabet hotel I am sleeping inside a colour.
A sound.
A letter.
I am sleeping inside all of the shapes containing this word.
In the alphabet hotel I am sleeping inside a sound.
A letter.
A shape.
I am sleeping inside, waiting to be born.

Author's note: Le Pavillon des Lettres is a hotel in Paris with 26 rooms. Calling Oulipo to mind, each room is represented by a letter, and each letter represents a poet or writer. Room N is Nerval; Z is Zola.

THE POINT OF PAIN
SUSAN ROBERTSON

The point of pain
was touched
in the small images;
the abandoned shoe,
the discarded bag,
the bullet holes in the glass.

And the cameras were there
to record it all.
All the pain,
in all its detail.
Ubiquitous camera phones
held up to capture
that horror,
if they ever could.

And what kind of album
would these pictures fill?
What kind of audience
are they for?
To display to children
and tell them of that day?
To explain?
To hold as a memory
of pain
and horror?
To keep it locked in the mind
and eye
of those who were there,
and those who were not?

What questions shall be asked?
Would you like
to see
my
Photograph
Album?

SLOW MOVING SORROW, FRIDAY 13TH, PARIS
DAMIEN B. DONNELLY

In the supermarket
on Saturday
in the 14th
on the 14th
in numb November
in Paris, their Paris,
our Paris, my Paris,
people push grief
in comfortless
trolleys
down shadowed aisles
of silence, strangers
claiming their spaces
in solidarity,
in queues
of slow moving sorrow,
seeing shadow in places
where once there was light,
terror in crowds
where once
there was music
death in their streets
where once there was life.
In
a supermarket
in
the 14th
on the 14th,
as the numbers rise

on a Saturday morning,
there is nothing available
on a single shelf
to fill the void
of what we lost
in the night

.

It's
not the whole world
It's
not the end of the world
but it's far too far from a perfect world

.

#NousSommesParis

BIOGRAPHIES

Zata Banks is a Fellow of the Royal Society of Arts and a member of the Typographic Circle. She is a brand consultant, artist, and the founder of the influential research art project PoetryFilm. Her artworks focus on semiotics and range between neon, language, film and sound. Her work has been shown at Tate Britain, the ICA, Southbank Centre, Cannes Film Festival, Ruskin Gallery Cambridge, O Miami and CCCB Barcelona.

Margo Berdeshevsky was born in New York city and often writes in Paris. Her recent poetry manuscript was a finalist for the National Poetry Series, 2015. Her poetry collections *Between Soul & Stone* and *But a Passage in Wilderness* are available from Sheep Meadow Press. In Europe her work has been published in *The Poetry Review*, *The Wolf*, *Europe*, *Siècle 21*, and *Confluences Poétiques* and her 'Letters from Paris' can be found in Poetry international, at: http://pionline.wordpress.com/category/letters-from-paris/

Caroline Bracken's poems have been widely published and she was the winner of the 2013 Writing.ie/Anam Cara Poetry Competition and the 2015 iYeats Poetry Competition. She has been shortlisted in many other competitions including the Listowel and Bridport Prize, and was nominated for a Forward Prize this year in the Best Single Poem category. She has been shortlisted for the Over the Edge New Writer of the Year competition in 2016 and is currently working towards a first collection of poetry. She lives in County Wicklow, Ireland.

Simon Carver was born in Sheffield, South Yorkshire. He read English Language and Literature at the University of Liverpool and has spent the last three decades working in the British music industry. He currently lives in West Berkshire, with much of his time spent in London. Readings of his poetry are available on YouTube.

Damien B. Donnely was born in Dublin, Ireland. He originally moved to Paris in 1998, where he works as a pattern designer for various fashion brands. His work has been published in last year's Irish short story anthology *Second Chance*, the web journal *The Fable Online* and he was a featured poet in the first edition of *Firefly* magazine.

Sophie Fenella is a poet and a performer from London whose has been published by *Magma*, *The Morning Star*, *Rising*, *Nasty Little Press*, and *Thynks Publications*. Most recently, she was nominated for the Outspoken prize for poetry, and was the winner of the (un) natural poetry competition, in association with Nuffield Council on Biothetics and the performance poetry organisation Apples and Snakes.

Adele Fraser lives and writes in the mountains of Snowdonia, North Wales. Her work has been published by a number of magazines. She has a poem in Eyewear Publishing's sister anthology *#refugeeswelcome: Poems in a Time of Crisis.*

Sandra M Gilbert is the author of eight collections of verse, most recently *Aftermath* (2011). Among her numerous prose books are *Death's Door* (2006) and *The Culinary Imagination* (2015). She is currently at work on a new volume of poetry, *Saturn's Meal*.

George Hobson is an American priest in the Episcopal/Anglican Church. He has published two books of poetry in England: *Rumours of Hope* (Piquant Editions) and *Forgotten Genocides of the 20th Century* (Garod Books), a collective volume to which he contributed seven poems. His poem 'Sun-Patch' won Second Prize in the International Bridport Poetry Competition in 1995.

Christina Lux's poetry has appeared on National Public Radio in the US, in journals such as *Women's Studies Quarterly*, *Feminist Formations*, *North Dakota Quarterly*, and *The Delmarva Review*, and is forthcoming in *Introduction to Women's Studies* from Oxford University

Press. She was born in Pasadena, California and has lived throughout the U.S., as well as in Canada, France, and Cameroon. She is now based at the University of California, Merced.

Jim Mackintosh is a working poet based in Perthshire, Scotland and is the Poet-in-Residence for St Johnstone FC. His latest collection, *The Rubicon of Ash* was published in March of 2016.

Kate Noakes' fifth collection is *Tattoo on Crow Street* (Parthian, 2015). Her website, boomslangpoetry.blogspot.com, is archived by the National Library of Wales. She was elected to the Welsh Academy in 2011.

Susan Robertson is a Scottish poet living in Edinburgh. In 2009 her first published book was written as part of a Fire Safety Education initiative, *Danielle's Fireworks Night.*

Greg Santos is the author of *Rabbit Punch!* (DC Books, 2014) and *The Emperor's Sofa* (DC Books, 2010). His writing has appeared in *The Walrus, Geist, Vallum,* and *Cha: An Asian Literary Journal.* He is currently the poetry editor of *carte blanche* and was previously on the Poetry Editorial Staff for the Paris-based *Upstairs at Duroc* from 2010-2011.

Sally-Shakti Willow is researching for a practice-based PhD in utopian poetics and experimental writing at the University of Westminster, where she also works as a research assistant for the Contemporary Small Press project (www.thecontemporarysmallpress.com).

Andrew Shields is a Basler from Detroit. His first full-length poetry collection, *Thomas Hardy Listens To Louis Armstrong,* was published by Eyewear Publishing in 2015. His band Human Shields also released their first album in 2015, *Somebody's Hometown.*

Annette Skade has a degree in Ancient Greek and Philosophy from Liverpool University and an MA in Poetry Studies from Dublin City University. Her first collection *Thimblerig* was published following her receipt of the Cork Literary Review Manuscript prize in 2012. She won the Bailieborough Poetry Competition in 2013, 2nd prize in the Allingham Festival Poetry Competition in 2014, and was awarded 3rd place in the Basil Bunting Competition in 2015.

George Symonds has poems published in *#refugeeswelcome: Poems in a Time of Crisis* (Eyewear Publishing) and *Over Land, Over Sea* (Five Leaves). He blogs at www.guiltynation.wordpress.com.

Wynn Wheldon's most recent publications are a collection of poetry, *Private Places* (IDP, 2015) and a biography of his father, Huw Wheldon, *Kicking the Bar* (Unbound, 2016). He has reviewed books for *Ink Sweat and Tears, Iota, Lunar Poetry, The Observer, Sabotage* and *The Spectator*. He lived in Paris for three months in 1977. He was born and lives in London.

Lightning Source UK Ltd.
Milton Keynes UK
UKOW02f0449141216
289973UK00002B/12/P